Knock Knock Jokes

Edited by
VICTORIA FREMONT

Illustrated by
LARRY DASTE

DOVER PUBLICATIONS, INC.
Mineola, New York

Bibliographical Note

Knock Knock Jokes is a new work, first published by Dover Publications, Inc., in 1998.

International Standard Book Number: 0-486-40402-1

Manufactured in the United States of America
Dover Publications, Inc., 31 East 2nd Street, Mineola, N.Y. 11501

Note

Heard any good knock knock jokes lately? Here are 60 of our favorites, all with fun illustrations. Read them to yourself or out loud to your friends. You might even be able to make up some of your own original knock knock jokes (and do your own drawings to go with them!). So read on and enjoy.

Knock, knock.
Who's there?
Isadore.
Isadore who?
Isadore open or shut?

Knock, knock.
Who's there?
Debbie.
Debbie who?
Debbie stung me and it hurts!

Knock, knock.
Who's there?
Danielle.
Danielle who?
Danielle so loud. I can hear you!

K<small>nock</small>, knock.
Who's there?
Andy.
Andy who?
Andy cow jumped over the moon.

4

Knock, knock.
Who's there?
Shelby.
Shelby who?
Shelby coming round the mountain when she comes.

Knock, knock.
Who's there?
Ida.
Ida who?
Ida rung the bell but it didn't work.

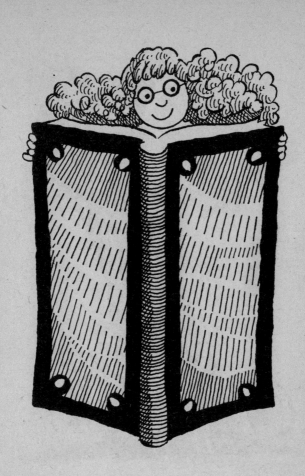

Knock, knock.
Who's there?
Rita.
Rita who?
Rita good book lately?

Knock, knock.
Who's there?
Ivan.
Ivan who?
Ivan to suck your blood!

Knock, knock.
Who's there?
Abby.
Abby who?
Abby birthday to you.

Knock, knock.
Who's there?
Sandy.
Sandy who?
Sandy Claus is coming to town.
10

Knock, knock.
Who's there?
Hugo.
Hugo who?
Hugo jump in the lake.

Knock, knock.
Who's there?
Radio.
Radio who?
Radio or not, here I come.

Knock, knock.
Who's there?
Genoa.
Genoa who?
Genoa good restaurant?

Knock, knock.
Who's there?
Freeze.
Freeze who?
Freeze a jolly good fellow.

Knock, knock.
Who's there?
Tree.
Tree who?
Tree blind mice, Tree blind mice.

Knock, knock.
Who's there?
Justin.
Justin who?
Justin the neighborhood and thought I'd say hello.
16

K nock, knock.
Who's there?
Anna.
Anna who?
Anna long came a spider and sat down beside her.

Knock, knock.
Who's there?
Wanda.
Wanda who?
Wanda what you're cooking for dinner.

Knock, knock.
Who's there?
Sarah.
Sarah who?
Sarah person in this house who owns this dog?

Knock, knock.
Who's there?
Edith.
Edith who?
Edith the right address? I may be lost.
20

Knock, knock.
Who's there?
Imus.
Imus who?
Imus tell you this secret!

Knock, knock.
Who's there?
Celia.
Celia who?
Celia letter before you mail it.

22

Knock, knock.
Who's there?
Howard.
Howard who?
Howard you like to come out and play?

Knock, knock.
Who's there?
Carrie.
Carrie who?
Carrie my luggage. It's too heavy.

Knock, knock.
Who's there?
Dishes.
Dishes who?
Dishes the pilot speaking.

Knock, knock.
Who's there?
Gladys.
Gladys who?
Gladys not raining out.
26

K nock, knock.
Who's there?
Anita.
Anita who?
Anita drink of water. It's hot out here.

Knock, knock.
Who's there?
Norma Lee.
Norma Lee who?
Norma Lee I use your bell, but it's broken.

Knock, knock.
Who's there?
Sid.
Sid who?
Sid down. Take a load off your feet.

Knock, knock.
Who's there?
Robin.
Robin who?
Robin is against the law.

30

Knock, knock.
Who's there?
Juan.
Juan who.
Juan to dance?

Knock, knock.
Who's there?
Carl.
Carl who?
Carl break down if you don't get it fixed.

Knock, knock.
Who's there?
Dexter.
Dexter who?
Dexter halls with boughs of holly.

Knock, knock.
Who's there?
Matthew.
Matthew who?
Matthew's so tight that I can't walk!

K nock, knock.
Who's there?
Stella.
Stella who?
Stella waiting for you to answer the door!

Knock, knock.
Who's there?
Bess.
Bess who?
*Bess to look through the peephole before answering
the door.*

36

Knock, knock.
Who's there?
Kenya.
Kenya who?
Kenya lend me a dollar?

.Knock, knock.
Who's there?
Avenue.
Avenue who?
Avenue got time for a cup of coffee?
38

Knock, knock.
Who's there?
Philip.
Philip who?
Philip the pitcher. I'm thirsty!

Knock, knock.
Who's there?
Tinkerbell.
Tinkerbell who?
Tinkerbell is out of order.

40

Knock, knock.
Who's there?
Timmy.
Timmy who?
Timmy it looks like rain.

Knock, knock.
Who's there?
Eddy.
Eddy who?
Eddy body want some ice cream?

42

Knock, knock.
Who's there?
Elsie.
Elsie who?
Elsie you later alligator.

Knock, knock.
Who's there?
Mickey.
Mickey who?
Mickey is stuck. Call a locksmith!
44

Knock, knock.
Who's there?
Harold.
Harold who?
Harold do you think I am?

Knock, knock.
Who's there?
Wheelbarrow.
Wheelbarrow who?
Wheelbarrow your keys since ours are lost.

Knock, knock.
Who's there?
Honey Bee.
Honey Bee who?
Honey Bee nice and answer the phone.

Knock, knock.
Who's there?
Ben.
Ben who?
Ben standing so long, my feet killing me.

48

Knock, knock.
Who's there?
Owl.
Owl who?
Owl be your friend till the end of time.

Knock, knock.
Who's there?
Lauren.
Lauren who?
Lauren order. You're under arrest!

Knock, knock.
Who's there?
Rocko.
Rocko who?
Rocko bye baby.

Knock, knock.
Who's there?
Saul.
Saul who?
Saul's there is, there is no more.
52

Knock, knock.
Who's there?
Fortification.
Fortification who?
Fortification we're going to Miami.

Knock, knock.
Who's there?
Irish.
Irish who?
Irish I were in love again.

54

Knock, knock.
Who's there?
Artie.
Artie who?
Artie trees green?

Knock, knock.
Who's there?
Sadie.
Sadie who?
Sadie pledge of allegiance.

Knock, knock.
Who's there?
Ida.
Ida who?
Ida come sooner, but I got stuck in traffic.

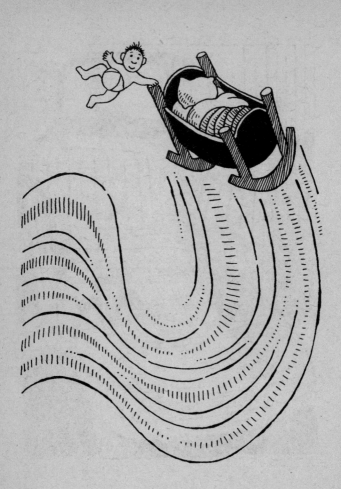

Knock, knock.
Who's there?
Wendy.
Wendy who?
Wendy wind blows, the cradle will rock.
58

K nock, knock.
Who's there?
Sheila.
Sheila who?
Sheila be there when the band starts playing!

K nock, knock.
Who's there?
Ken.
Ken who?
Ken you come out and play?